More praise for *Spirit Spout*

Devon Balwit's *Spirit Spout* – a poetic vision directly engaging with Melville's *Moby-Dick; or, The Whale* – is an eschatological tour de force. The poet practices an intertextual jouissance showcasing singular gifts for sound and image. We encounter "the thrown gauntlet // the poking prod of the devil's own advocate"; there is salt, wind, brine and ocean; Melville as god, as demon; Melville in the throes of creation and also grieving. Ishmael, Ahab, and Queequeg beckon. Both travelogue and existential reckoning with life, there is a painterly attention to the physical, to the body; there is a grappling with sociology and philosophy: "Our thinking // always butting up against the ribs / of the paradigms we travel in." Balwit's powers are on full display – this book's spirit is deep and wide. — **Charles Kell**, author of *Ishmael Mask*

Spirit Spout

Devon Balwit

Nixes Mate Books
Allston, Massachusetts

Copyright © 2023 Devon Balwit

Book design by d'Entremont

Cover photograph used with permission.

All rights reserved. This book or any portion thereof may not be reproduced or used in any manner whatsoever without the express written permission of the publisher except for the use of brief quotations in a book review or scholarly journal.

All quotations from Herman Melville's *Moby Dick; or, The Whale*

ISBN 978-1-949279-45-0

Nixes Mate Books
POBox 1179
Allston, MA 02134
nixesmate.pub

To Fritz, Xander, Avital, and Theo,
who have been an excellent crew as I chase my whales.

Contents

I Go Willingly	3
The Best We Can Do Now for the Head Is to Pray Heaven the Tackles May Hold	4
Fast Fish / Loose Fish	6
Fast at Both Ends: A Golden Shovel	8
Self-Consciousness, or The Whale	9
Trouble in the Blood	13
A Cunning and Most Feline Thing	14
The Raft	15
How is Mortal Man to Account for It?	16
Ahab's Magnet	17
Castaway	20
Say What Ye Will, Shipmate	21
This Woman Votes to Keep Melville in the Canon	23
Heel	24
Fashioning Vastness	26
The Catch	27
Iron Nails	28
A Wild Vindictiveness	30
Coiled Away	31
Queequeg's Ramadan	32
Was There Ever Such Unconsciousness?	33
I Am Ready to Squeeze Case Eternally	34
Chasing Leviathan	36
Sailor's Log	38

Phrenology / Philology	39
Bound	41
Selfie	43
All Aleak	44
She Goes Down Rollicking	45
That Audacious Staff	47
Where I Belong	48
Burning One's Own Body: An Abecedarian	50
Food of Light	52
Something that Can Hold	53
At Work in Us	54
Nothing More Than	55
Landfall: A Golden Shovel	56
The Line	58
Spirit Spout	59
Starbuck's Lament	61
The Voice of My Conscience Takes Rare Delight	63
The Bow Must Bear the Brunt	64
Subtle Demonisms	65
Thou Did'st Not Know Ahab Then	67
No Key	69
Dismasted and Re-	70
That Imbecile Candle	72
Now You Know	73
The Black Bubble	74
Last Sleep	75

Spirit Spout

I Go Willingly

[T]his is my substitute for pistol and ball.

Ships differ but little, freeboard and draw.
Supine in my berth, the deck presses
my face like a palm. I go willingly
when called to the watch. In the crow's nest,
at least I can breathe as I shoulder
the void. Aren't I always searching
for obstacles or opportunities, hull-gnawing
crags or a mass of flesh to be rendered?
My lot tends toward superstition, albatross
and St Elmo's fire, vast medusae afloat
on phosphorescent blooms. Even aloft,
sail unclewed, I swoon at the fragility
of it all, 80 tons of flesh not enough to protect
the whale, the earth itself but a child's globe
awaiting a knock. Unlike many, I relish
captain and mate, pulling on orders
like comfortable sleeves. Tell me what to do
till I drop, I say, my body so tired
I no longer awaken at the threat of death,
so tired the mind snuffs out like a candle.

The Best We Can Do Now for the Head Is to Pray Heaven the Tackles May Hold

It must be borne in mind that all this time we have a Sperm Whale's prodigious head hanging to the Pequod's side. But we must let it continue hanging there a while until we can get a chance to attend to it.

Delicately, we look elsewhere, avoiding
the obvious, the conjoined twin, the scars raised

like quilt seams, the missing limb. It's not
that we aren't curious. We're dying to run

our fingers where the two meet, to ask *why*
and *when* and *how* and fondle the pink stump,

but we've been properly brought up and so
crease and pleat conversation into dainty

geometrics, a Mughal privacy screen. We draw
our knees in tight so as not to disturb the elephant,

all the while mesmerized by his tufted hide.
We hint with the intensity of our gaze, like one

feeling for the spring to a hidden compartment.
What we'd find there were it to release

might be nothing more than a mirror
reflecting our own frightful deformity.

Fast Fish / Loose Fish

What are the Rights of Man and the Liberties of the World but Loose-Fish? What all men's minds and opinions but Loose-Fish? ...What to the ostentatious smuggling verbalists are the thoughts of thinkers but Loose-Fish? ... And what are you, reader, but a Loose-Fish and a Fast-Fish, too?

Though you would have it so,
        you are no freer

than a harpooned whale.
        You run with the lines

hurled into you at birth
        and tightening therefrom,

pricked by well-wrought barbs
        and skilled whalers

who know your hungers, your habits,
        your limits.

Flap flukes in protest, batter your head
        against the stalking boats,

but still you're bound. Or—
    temporarily loose—

you dangle lances, a cutting spade,
    from a hempen tangle,

bobbing in place, alive
    yet drowning.

You dream of being unfettered,
    but were you so,

you'd only flounder, circling
    other pods or other prisoners,

so wanting to be wanted
    that even hunted would suffice.

Fast at Both Ends: A Golden Shovel

...it must be said that the monkey-rope was fast at both ends; fast to Queequeg's broad canvas belt, and fast to my narrow leather one. So that for better or for worse, we two, for the time, were wedded; and should poor Queequeg sink to rise no more, then both usage and honor demanded that instead of cutting the cord, it should drag me down in his wake.

Scoot your knees as far away from mine as you please; this
still won't stop us from touching. Our situation
is almost as bad as the conjoined. Yank the rug out from one of
us, and the other falls. Poison your well, and mine
gives bitter water. No one was
thinking. No one considered *what ifs*. Now, the
man in front plummets, and each of us slides. The situation
couldn't be direr. Of
course, we scrabble to undo the knots, but already we are unbalanced, every
second borrowed. Now do you feel mortal
terror? And what of our legacy? That
we must cobble together as we hurtle: the fate of everyone that breathes.

Self-Consciousness, or The Whale

> *...he seemed entirely at his ease; preserving the utmost serenity; content with his own companionship; always equal to himself.*

I. Biographical

You start where you start and then proceed,
        certain, like everyone, that you

were adopted, the lost child of nobility. Eventually,
        you realize yourself tethered by blood

to the screamers you live with, neck tendons
        straining just as they did

begetting you. You imprint on certain songs
        like a snow goose following a man

flapping across a field in a canvas armature.
        You tick off firsts, first crush, first kiss,

first toke, first job, first fuck, all done badly. You repeat:
        the future will liberate me.

Unlike a dragonfly, however, you do not rise, iridescent.

    Rather, each instar stunts you further,

wings dropping off and eyes bulging. You clack
    your mandibles and sink deeper into mud.

II. Ahab

You cultivate crazy, your own persistent
    obsessions, google your name to learn

that the first face that appears pegs you
    for an aged drunk, crepe-skinned

and slurring, a mugshot the curious will see,
    no way to remove it. As ever, destiny

drags you down like the retreating rumor
    of a whale. You know the darkness.

III. Wheelbarrow

The street people push their world before them
    in carts, rattling their approach

like ancient lepers. You can choose

    to cross or stand your ground, unafraid.

What you fear isn't them, but awkwardness.
    Where to look? –

as at an interview, when the candidate
    has his zipper down or food

between his teeth. These people know
    they are homeless. They intuit

your inner roil, guessing that you have forgotten
    your glasses darken in the light

and that you imagine them staring
    into your very soul.

IV: Forecastle—Midnight

You prowl the cutting-edge of night,
gritty-eyed as the bowsprit spears
the hours, the whole craft creaking

as it breathes, the shifting sea oily
and restless. You seek to appease the dark
gods, swearing you are no Jonah.

V: Queequeg in His Coffin

The mother holds her son by the hood.
A new walker, he stutter-steps, speeds

and slows, and veers off course. How gently
she guards him from overreaching. Still

unsteady, you work to keep yourself
from the same, one hand against your nape,

a firm pressure upward. You do not want
sit or be carried. You are not ready.

Trouble in the Blood

> *...let Ahab beware of Ahab; beware of thyself, old man.*

Some days your every move wafts rot;
you dream of cauterizing rods, of ready lancets.

To look at you, nothing seems awry, your fester
buried like magma in crust, your weapon holstered.

Melville was similarly glum. His wife tired of it,
and his eldest took his own life with a bullet,

a hereditary trouble in the blood. Wise salts
say it's better to turn towards tumult

than to let it press you from behind, so you lean,
groaning into the gale of your Cape Horn.

Oddly, port is worse, others' merriment
a torment. You carry your own weather, bent

muttering over your glass. Others skirt you wide,
warned, as if by a beacon, of the rocks you hide.

A Cunning and Most Feline Thing

*Human madness is oftentimes a cunning and most feline thing.
When you think it fled, it may have but become transfigured into
some still subtler form.*

Mine waits till Saturday to take off its disguises,
knowing that Sunday follows, a day of even greater stasis.

Then, stripped of false civility, it loves to pull
at time, stretching it like taffy beyond its normal

measure. Into this abyss, it drops me, hands frozen
like the clock, alone and mournful, into a blue zone,

the walls of my crevasse sheer all the way up
to the thinnest sliver of sky. It will not stop

playing me on its rope until the planet wheels
twice, Monday come again, fixing me upon its rails.

The Raft

It was the whiteness of the whale that above all things appalled me.

What is it, after all, but a raft
of associations, us

tossed from our mother ship
and clinging for dear life?

Letting go means being borne
under, while holding spins us

in rudderless circles. Ignorant
of everything but our bit

of real estate, we forget
the nudibranchs, the rainbow-hued

flatworms, the anglerfish fluorescing
impossible candles.

How is Mortal Man to Account for It?

[T]here yet lurks an elusive something in the innermost idea of this hue

Ishmael, the whale's eyes are placed so it cannot see
itself. It doesn't know of its uncanny

pallor. Its notions come from listening to other whales
and concluding how it too must be. Small

wonder it blunders, then feels the punishing
harpoon-thrusts in its hide before fleeing

back to safer solitude. There
it's just another denizen of murk,

shielded from peering and positing.
How is mortal man to account for it, our thinking

always butting up against the ribs
of the paradigms we travel in, crib

to grave? Am I alone in wanting the whale
to escape even its most storied whaler?

Ahab's Magnet

I: The Mast-Head

Hand over hand, I have uphauled me,
fighting a certain leadenness of soul.

Now, I pendulum beneath sky like
the stylus of an automaton, scribing

the air with daydreams. I am both
smaller than ever I was and vaster,

a pepper-speck in God's broth-bowl,
and the inhale of universal lungs.

II: Surmise

What within your breast burns?
        There's naught to see, so I

must wager. I watch at what and where
        your nostrils flare and when

your face flushes. I watch your fingers
    furl into fists. Inside

their clench, coals glare, baleful.
    You must release the sear

and bare yourself to the watchful.
    Yes, I listen to your *laus perennis*,

your prayer perpetual, asking always
    for one thing:

the delivery into your hands
    of the hunted.

III: The Life-Buoy

Drowning, we reach. It matters little
    for what, even the living

pushed below us, just to raise
    our nostrils an inch

above the swell. A caulked barrel,
    a pitch-seamed coffin,

we'll use whatever flotsam bobs
      in answer to our gasping.

Castaway

The intense concentration of self in the middle of such a heartless immensity, my God! who can tell it?

Like Pip, we float on a horizonless sea,
ringed by immensity. Some fail to see

it, imagining their whaleboat the world,
distracted and distracting in their revelry, startled

into truth only by age, illness, or poverty.
Is it better, like Pip, to be educated early?

Castaway, we take the shape of dead men.
Will it be tooth or terror that does us in?

Terror marks us either way, the hours
spent with only ourselves for comfort, failures

at ministry and uplift. When our fellows finally spot
and fish us up, we are worse for wear. Not

even rum can stop our muttering – *God's foot
treadles the loom, and faithless us to tell it.*

Say What Ye Will, Shipmate

Say what ye will, shipmate; I've sharp ears.
Aye, you are the chap, ain't ye, that heard the hum of the old Quakeress's
knitting needles fifty miles at sea from Nantucket.

Yes, yes, all my senses painfully acute
and to those fashioned otherwise, impossible

to credit, like one suffering Lyme Disease,
long-Covid, or Fibromyalgia. I tell you every doubt

pointed my direction smites me, needling
through fascia like slivers from a blast.

Someday, though, just as Fedallah and his crew
rose, blinking, from Ahab's hold, so too

Borrelia burgdorferi will appear
in the blood draw, or anxiety

in the brain, every able-bodied soul
struck dumb by hard evidence.

Didn't I hear 'em in the hold?
I'll say of the emerging strangers.

Aye, you'll need to concede.
You most certainly did.

This Woman Votes to Keep Melville in the Canon

[W]here's your girls?

You can count them on one hand: Mrs. Hussey
ladling chowder in the Try Pots, Captain Bildad's sister

in port, delivering spare harpoons, a nightcap, and a Bible.
Some of the men have wives at home, others, memories

of female comfort in a distant port, but you'll not see any
women aboard, taking a turn with the holystone or peering

from the crow's nest. None are lancers, none reef sails.
Still, I find myself both forward and aft. I know obsession,

superstition, and work's hypnotism. Like Starbuck,
I fret over plots I lack strength to bring to fruition

and feel nostalgia for a self I'll never revisit. Like Tashtego,
I cry out at midnight for rum. I spring leaks, awaken

to every compass demagnetized by storm, and yet, an Ahab,
refuse to change course or lay anchor. Like Stubb, I laugh

because a laugh's the wisest, easiest answer to all that's queer.
Sometimes the other is the truest mirror.

Heel

[E]ven blackness has its brilliancy...

White, I can't know how Pip's description reads
to one who is Black, but imagine it similar

to when I turn a page and stumble
over the goyim's Jews, oily and money-grubbing,

loud and embarrassingly familiar. Even one possessing
the pleasant, genial, jolly brightness peculiar

to one's tribe might lose it at being told so
by an outsider. White Ishmael shares Queequeg's bed

and pipe, notes his kingly manners, hygiene,
and his devotion to his creed, but makes too much of it,

like one vaunting his ally-ship, BLM sign
given pride of place on the lawn, his presence

at protests tallied hash-tagged selfies. Better
than the opposite, at least, or the ones who think

by not mentioning difference, the difference
disappears. Better to have our Procrustean bed

out in the open where we can take its measure
and guffaw: *So that's what you think of us—better*

than many but leaving much to be desired.
A stink affixed to the bootheel of genius.

Fashioning Vastness

The hours wore on; --Ahab now shut up within his cabin; anon, pacing the deck, with the same intense bigotry of purpose in his aspect.

Oblivious to my deformity, I call them to me
and pace the deck.

Between thumb and forefinger, I burnish my doubloon:
This is knowledge! This, purpose!

But they raise no huzzah as I nail it to the masthead,
tip no harpoons to our mutual success.

Instead, they wait for me to exhaust myself,
releasing them again to their hammocks.

All night, I listen to dark water, trying to distill
persuasion from the rushing.

It's like this, I say, fashioning vastness
with pallid hands.

More snickers and troughs, nudges and salt spray.
By the end, I shall be quite cured.

The Catch

Benthic and alien, I muscle my concerns
up and down the banks of desks, from one side

of the board to the other, seeking to provoke
language from whatever current obsession

rules me in the pre-dawn darkness. Pelagic,
they stare, blowing bubbles, gills

mechanically at work, finlike fingers
still on an empty page, nothing I say

interesting enough to note. As if deprived
of air, I grow increasingly frantic,

flapping and straining against the hook,
which must be time, tugging me

from view. Yes, they just have to wait
me out, and I will vanish, leaving them

to roll their eyes and rejoin their shoal
while, sidelined, I am iced and gutted.

Iron Nails

> *I see in him outrageous strength, with an inscrutable malice sinewing it.*

You say I rant, inventing demons
where there are none, but the world
is thick with devils. Perhaps I am

a magnet to malice, an invisible
pull leading ever to my bitter
mouthful. Why would I make

this up, what gain from it?
For me, there is no sleep to knit
the raveled sleeve, no pause

in my distress. People look askance
and cross to the other side, pulling
their children close as I draw near.

A lone albatross, I wear Cain's mark
upon my brow, a blood-splash
that sets me ever in tracklessness

with the owls and the night-
scrabblers. I rave the way ordinary objects
fall earthwards, compelled.

I'd strike the sun if it insulted me.
And so it does, leering and all-seeing.
The path to my fixed purpose is set

with iron nails, whereon my soul
is grooved to run. What can a train do
but scream as it passes?

A Wild Vindictiveness

> *Small reason was there to doubt, then, that ever since that almost fatal encounter, Ahab had cherished a wild vindictiveness against the whale, all the more fell for that in his frantic morbidness he at last came to identify with him, not only all his bodily woes, but all his intellectual and spiritual exasperations.*

Here is where I am, not in the silvery
palmed slab. *Here*, a thing of terrible
and wrecked glory, not sexy but hoary.
Stop and pay witness to the inevitable.
Put your goddamn phones down!
Be bored a moment. Yes, I mean bored,
the sullen weight of you, your sad self, grown
and growing heavier company by the hour, hard-
pressed to sit in solemnity as at a wake.
Do I annoy you? Good. Tell me why
in a three-paged composition. Make
every word count. I hear your sighs
and raise you one, my own, loud as a gale,
the anguished cry of a long-tormented soul.

Coiled Away

> *He's the devil, I say. The reason why you don't see his tail, is because he tucks it up out of sight; he carries it coiled away in his pocket...*

Cloven hooves booted, tail tucked,
the devil looks the very picture

of you or me, indeed, could be,
for what do we know

of each other's private tantrums.
We're mostly princely

in our manners, bright day
bookending our squalls.

And when we're evil, is it by nature
or provocation? I believe the jury

hung, the very webbing
of our fingers and toes mottled.

Queequeg's Ramadan

> *I began to grow vexed with him; it seemed so downright senseless and insane to be sitting there all day and half the night on his hams in a cold room, holding a piece of wood on his head.*

I both envy and belittle your devotion.
My own comes and goes like weather.

Try as I might, I cannot keep my idols
from toppling although I yearn

to orient myself towards something, if only
that sacred emptiness through which light sends

its transitory beam. I want to think
faith good, more than a gavel, a rock, a pit,

a pyre demanding sacrifice. I, too, long
to lose myself in prayer, to invoke

whatever would unlock my self-conceit
and free what love remains in me.

Was There Ever Such Unconsciousness?

The poor bumpkin was restored. All hands voted Queequeg a noble trump;
the captain begged his pardon.

God, his popularity bothers me,
term after term, the reams of praise

I must sort and file, while the words
used for me scald, worse

because I know the truth
of our disparity, hunched over

myself, nursing slights that snag
before rending the whole garment.

He, in contrast, arrives
brimming love. Some inner light,

something more than blood
runs in his veins, constantly replenishing.

How like Cain I feel, fleeing before
smallness becomes my undoing.

I Am Ready to Squeeze Case Eternally

Squeeze! Squeeze! Squeeze! all the morning long. I squeezed that sperm until I myself almost melted into it; I squeezed that sperm until...I found myself unwittingly squeezing my co-laborers' hands in it, mistaking their hands for the gentle globules.

I love you, and you too, you bastards.
You who never respond in kind

and wouldn't greet me on the street.
Still, I am yours. I love your great,

insufferable boasting, your vaunting
of yourself until you swell like leviathan

in the blue. I make your bragging
my own: the prizes and the publications,

the workshops and professorships.
I share your victories and congratulations.

Did you ever dream we would become
one flesh, my insignificance and your greatness?

There, in the spotlight, can you feel
the gentle pressure of my admiration?

Squeeze! Squeeze! Squeeze!
Like Ishmael, I could do this all day,

unctuous before the try-works.
May you never lose your brainpan excess,

our excuse for a lovefest, afloat,
as we are, on an indifferent sea.

Chasing Leviathan

I. Ambergris

You pass through the body, through the body
      turning musky sweet with time

a diaphanous smoke, a wax, a covetousness.
      You gather in the gut, in the gut

a grip, a roiling of swell, a rotten salt-stink
      reborn as unguent. You ease

the passage, ease the passage of the rough
      and the rasping, the flaying,

the flensing. You bob in the solitary, bob
      in the solitary, caught up

in current, in the shrugging of the world's
      shoulders. Finally, you beach,

you beach on the wrack-line, coughed up,
      shat out, a priceless clot.

II. Pitchpoling

Birthed to swim, you swam, nuzzling
       thick cream from the salty teat,

learning to listen at the lowest register,
       to follow deep current

to faraway singers. But all around writhed
       small grubs with iron lances,

blood hungry, eager to render, creeping
       alongside and spearing heart-deep.

Pricked, you gouted, unspooling
       in red-spouted flight

until you became no more
       than casked fat.

III. The Crotch

Wherein rests the harpoon, wherein rests the prick,
wherein lies danger, wherein nestles chance and

chance's second, which may be full, or which may
be empty, which awaits the battle's spare geometry.

Sailor's Log

Melville saw a man plunge into the sea
and threw him tackle, which he dropped, smiling as he sank,
the jump intentional, his chosen way to free
himself from suffering. As the ship's sails shrank
on the horizon, he let himself go down
as a means of rising. Others plummeted from a moment's
inattention, wailing as they left the shrouds, a sound
that needled every heart, and deeper, as impatient
captains halted the search, no body to be found.
Storms toppled ships or set survivors
hopelessly adrift. What finally washed aground
was but a fragment of keel, cask, or collar.
So many ways, then, that we cease to be,
and so few who stop and note our journey.

Phrenology / Philology

*Champollion deciphered the wrinkled granite hieroglyphics.
But there is no Champollion to decipher the Egypt of every man's and
every being's face.*

But not for want of trying, the untiring
reading of grimace and grin, the learned

lexicon of squint. To survive, the wise
lover notes the barometry of a forehead

and remembers its weather – *Red sky
at morning, sailors take warning; red sky*

at night, sailors delight – and other such
to avoid squalls. Each new partner demands

a Rosetta Stone, that we take what we know
and parse what is strange for a key –

this when cut off in traffic, this
when gainsaid, when thwarted, when flattered,

marked in columns and revisited
by lamplight. By trial and error, we move

between papyrus and cartouche,
the grammar of yesterday and tomorrow.

Bound

> *The Fin-Back is not gregarious. He seems a whale-hater, as some men are man-haters... always going solitary; unexpectedly rising to the surface in the remotest and most sullen waters; his straight and single lofty jet rising like a tall misanthropic spear upon a barren plain.*

You purposely slow to lift your middle finger,
a misanthropic spear. All its target did

was nose blindly into traffic, a near miss.
I remonstrate as I always do, begging you

to move beyond invective, to separate yourself
from those who thunder *Kill them all*.

I know myself too black a pot to criticize
your bellicose kettle, can only retreat

into aggrieved silence, listening to some unseen
guitarist's dominants and light harmonics.

As we turn into the parking garage, I smile
at an exiting stranger. She smiles, also,

from a face of burnished copper. Does this cancel out
your earlier cursing? Too soon to say. The day

must be entered, me committing to its waters
before I sound them. Leaving the car, I pause

a moment as if to wave a tiny truce flag.
Your head in the trunk, you, most likely,

do not see. We move off with a flick of fins
to our concerns: sullen, solitary, bound.

Selfie

Woe to him who seeks to please rather than to appall!

I see you, you butter-dripping flatterer,
liming the corpses, spackling over rot

reaching deep to foundation, see you
posing before the skinny mirror,

strewing likes and emoticons, polishing
scuffs till they shine to blinding, know

you for a laudatory lickspittle, drool-wiper,
photo-shopper, redactor, a head-nodding ass-

kisser, fawning over the naked emperor
and his whole entourage; I see you bolting

from the approach of jackboots, the rumble
of the windowless vans, see you double-

chaining the door and cowering behind
the dropped shutters of my own eyes.

All Aleak

I'm all aleak myself. Aye! leaks in leaks! not only full of leaky casks, but those casks are in a leaky ship…yet I don't stop to plug my leak; for who could find it in the deep-loaded hull; or how hope to plug it, even if found, in this life's howling gale?

Every day a worse battering, planks fighting their form
        and straining the nails. Even a bird,

hollow-boned atop a rail, unbalances. I bail,
        sending the brackish overboard.

Which cask is it? Damned if I know. Most likely,
        none are true,

and it's been a slow seeping all along,
        secrets beading at the seams

down in the hold's darkness. Mid-voyage,
        what other course

but to jerry-rig, anything to keep from foundering?
        Nights, I dream of it,

the canting of the deck and the sound of water
        rushing through hatchways.

She Goes Down Rollicking

[Flask] goes down rollicking, so far at least as he remains visible from the deck...but ere stepping into the cabin doorway below, he pauses, ships a new face altogether.

Flask, I'm your type, full of beans and bluster
until the captain enters, whereupon

I solemnize, liking my secure leavings
enough to forego my beloved butter

if it isn't handed to me. I admire the Queequegs,
who remain kingly through and through,

wearing the same face when sucking on their pipe
as when confronting ignorance. So much themselves,

they care nothing for how they seem.
They inspire great loyalty

while we'll have to sing our own praises
and write our own short epitaphs.

*And had Flask helped himself, the chances were
Ahab had never so much as noticed it.*

So near we sit to satisfaction, then,
my twin, did we dare snatch it.

Our false rollicking reveals us hungry,
with smiles that never reach our eyes.

That Audacious Staff

I rejoice in my spine, as in the firm audacious staff of that flag which I fling half out to the world.

Sometimes, I want to swing a quick arc and shatter, a display of mood or temper that ends in fragments—but there it is, what prevents me, some moor or tether that balks when I try to stray as far as madness wishes, reducing dare smaller than thought and paler – call it spine, or call it an invisible perimeter like a dog fence, synched to an unseen collar and paining at approach, marking me chordate and keeping me upright, snapped at by breezes.

Where I Belong

> *While their masters, the mates, seemed afraid of the sound of the hinges of their own jaws, the harpooners chewed their food with such a relish that there was a report to it.*

Never mistake me for measured or modulated,
      bit between teeth and properly reined.

Instead, my steps slap with a head-turning echo;
      when I guffaw, crowns catch light.

Excuse me from the state dinner, napkin on lap
      and silverware properly employed.

Set me, instead, a plate amongst the reachers
      and the lip-smackers, where soup

spatters shirtfronts, and full glasses tumble
      to gesticulation, further puddling

the crumb-covered table. Not for me the auction
      with its discreet nods and uplifted

paddles, but rather the bellowing of likes
      and dislikes, the thrown gauntlet,

the poking prod of the devil's own advocate.
    Not the cheek-busk, the air kiss,

or the elbow squeeze, but the huzzah and the bawdy
    wink. Neither allusion nor euphemism,

but an anatomy lesson complete with gestures
    underscoring how and where and with what

verve. Yoke me with the fearless harpooners,
    all keen blade and keener appetite.

Burning One's Own Body: An Abecedarian

Like a plethoric burning martyr, or a self-consuming misanthrope, once ignited, the whale supplies his own fuel and burns by his own body.

Athwart goes the body, from which
blankets of blubber are stripped by the whaling spades, un-
curling skywards on hooks while,
down below, the crew works the windlass,
everyone straining to tear the blanket of
flesh free from the carcass. Descendent
goes the rind, sliced through, while up
heaves that part still unfurling
in a perfect synchrony of
jobs done and redone until their
knowing is intuited.
Like Starbuck and Stubb, I flense my whale –
Melville – who releases in coils, a
necessary violence to get at the
oil that illuminates my
pitchiest nights. My whale is unarguably, un-
questionably greater than any Sperm or
Right ever recorded, offering a rendering that
stops only if I say "enough!" My
try-works bubble and bubble

under my desk, my deck, in a Stygian
vision. O how I smoke and scorch,
wielding my pronged fork, my keyboard keys,
x-ing out and filling in, over and over, until
you, my reader, become desperate to flee the Ahabian
zeal of me.

Food of Light

> *[B]ut the whaleman, as he seeks the food of light, so he lives in light...*

How can I prove to my students that although I am cash-poor,
I am rich, *in the pitchiest night, still housing an illumination?*

Although empty of pocket, I am glutted with thoughts
that glow, a surfeit of all the words they resist

as lacking in utility. No one really talks like this,
they challenge me. I do, and let that be a lesson to them,

fulminating like Isaiah in their midst, my mouth afire.
Look at the world, I say, girdled round, sunrise and sunset.

Even the blazing forests of the west ruddy us. Poetry?
Their lips curl. I look past them, past the schoolroom wall

to my desk, to where I see Ahab's ocean in the sky,
Ishmael clinging to the rooftops as to Queequeg's coffin.

It's so bright I have to squint. Why,
I rarely sleep for the shine of it.

Something that Can Hold

Oh, sir, it will break bones—beware, beware!
No fear; I like a good grip; I like to feel something in this slippery world
that can hold, man.

The contest rules discourage poetry—who
reads it, after all? A versifying friend
begs for patrons. Even I refuse,
for how to fund just one? If I lend
to her, there's fifty more beside. And still –
I write it. What's wrong with me? Like Ahab,
I crave the bone-cracking pinch, the soul-
searing flicker, a light-daub into the drab
routine. A small fish and pale, I keep
my day-job, polishing the dull blades
racking the aisles. Yes, I confess I weep
some nights for the waste of it. I wasn't made
to love the remedial. Home, I stick a finger
in and tighten the screws. I let the pain linger.

At Work in Us

> *Though, in overseeing the pursuit of this whale, Captain Ahab had evinced his customary activity…yet now that the creature was dead, some vague dissatisfaction, or impatience, or despair seemed working in him.*

The caught thing is never the one wished for.
Its mere succumbing proves it lesser.

It has the wrong dimensions, smaller in the hand,
oddly, than when seen from afar, and what seemed

iridescence proves but a trick of light.
Out it goes on trash night.

And despite the persistence of the dream,
its crisp outline bleeds as if daubed. Some

witchery keeps it forever in retreat. Or perhaps
death, patiently smirking, dismissive of any stops

along the way, knowing recognition but a reprieve,
all of us mere slurry in the restive

tectonics of time. So, customary activity, yes,
that dogged pursuit of the hopeless.

Nothing More Than

You is sharks, sartin; but if you gobern de shark in you, why den you be angel; for all angel is not'ing more dan de shark well goberned.

Like Ishmael, only the thinnest hull
separates me from the sharks

slapping tails against the midnight
hull, tearing mouthfuls of a carcass

awaiting rendering. Each time I drowse,
plank-thunks startle me upright. Ghost

shadows dance in the lamp's flicker.
I listen to the feasting, the slosh

of salt brine against staves. Hands
to the rough walls, I sand my fears

until their rasp quiets, until the glutted
feeders return to the deeps. By morning

dread resolves into task. Obedient, I put
one foot in front of the other, an angel

nothing more a shark, well-governed.
I govern myself, a speck amidst swells.

Landfall: A Golden Shovel

*Few or no words were spoken; and the silent ship, as if manned
by painted sailors in wax, day after day tore on through the swift
madness and gladness of the demoniac waves.*

Aging and anxious, I sleep badly, just a few
hours of respite before the brain's door clatters wide in wind, or
a rustle from the garden sets in motion its ungreased machinery. No
baths or teas or breathing diminishes the torrent of words
and attendant emotions, the body's bullies. Whatever were
the day's worst errors resurrect, each utterance spoken
in impatience or anger. The future skulks, and
a distant train whistles through the
city's crossings. These are the hours given to silent
scavenging. Coons and possums creep from their bark ship
to prowl the yards and tangle with cats as
if the dark itself were belligerent. If
they were to lift their heads, they'd see my window, manned,
Cyclopean. I will return to the day, gritty-eyed, fueled by
caffeine and doggedness. If I am lucky, I will have painted
a record of my slow journey, like sailors'
scrimshaw or wayfarers' cairns, something to justify restiveness. In

the morning, everything that looms diminishes, candle-wax
congealed to droplets on the chipped plate. The day
stands with hands on hips, asking *Really?* After
the awful creep of the clock, I don't even mind. Let the day
scold; anything is better than the dark chorus that tore
me upright. The first bird announces 3:58. On
cue, another joins; a car passes. I have made it through
and stand on the beach upright, corpses splayed all
around. Shaking, urinous, I rejoin my company, the
normal and purpose-driven. Swift
motions mark routine and pull a curtain over madness.
I lose myself in business and
pretend the next night will never come. Gladness
battles weariness. I take out the dog, collect the paper, read of
problems that dwarf my own. The
world restores its mask and hides its demoniac
face. From the shore, I have no fear of waves.

The Line

Umbilical coil, it tethers to the mothership, fifteen strands wound round, three times spliced, plunges with the plummeting hundreds of fathoms, ribboning behind the flung lance. Herky-jerking all, it yanks grizzled and greenhorn, chatter-toothed and rib-rattled. Each tries his best to remain untangled, for the rope loves an ankle as well as a fin, cares nothing for breath, nothing for its first makers. At day's end, either it returns, greased, to its tub, or it drifts through dark current trailing a fringe of the drowned.

Spirit Spout

Ahab dozes in his captain's chair,
    shut eyes fixed fast to the tell-tale.

Even in sleep, he orients himself to the compass
    of his obsession,

following its spirit spout through his dreams,
    knuckles white to the tiller.

Burning blubber lifts a sweet stink to his nostrils,
    immune to the judgement

of his fellows, their sideways glances
    of scorn or pity. Quiet as a shipboard cat,

you circle him round, knife at the ready.
    One quick cut, and all could turn

for the nearest port. You'd be in irons,
    but you'd die aground, be buried in it.

You want to crack him like a coconut, drain
    his brainpan of its white infection.

What curse squats upon you, Starbuck,
    to place you here? There's no praying

it free; you've tried. You'll have to play
    your line to its end.

Your hilt hand trembles. The old man
    mumbles and snores.

Starbuck's Lament

Will I, nill I, the ineffable thing has tied me to him

I, who only ever wanted a *bayt nour*,
a house of light, green hills rolling

lavender in the gloaming, and children
rolling, too, in play, a loyal dog at the heel,

a wife, warm-hearted and warm between
goose down, find myself, instead,

on balky swells, yoked to a madman. He,
my *bête noire*, tricks me ever-further

from my heart's desire and closer to his –
a chalky phantom that cares nothing

about his white-rimmed insomniac eye
that cares too much – breeching and then

retreating into darkness, busy about its own
purposes. Where my firm will? Where

the nay-sayer in me? Why was I born
to pull the forelock and say *Aye*, hoping

that the other would read in my silence
loud disavowal? *Beaten now*, I pen a last

testament that will never be sent, and
hug babe and bride in dreamtime only.

The Voice of My Conscience Takes Rare Delight

What will the owners say, sir?
...What cares Ahab? Owners, owners? Thou art always prating to me, Starbuck, about those miserly owners, as if the owners were my conscience.

Threaten me, will you? You'll tell the boss
I teach you things of little use? Go to it, then,

as if he didn't know already, our every conversation
plagued by hapax legomenon. Why drill what's common?

The world is passing strange, and you
should be able to name it thus, precisely. Think

what it means to reach into your pockets, able
to choose among gems. I'll not fill you with gravel

though I end up pitched on it. Even a boot
in the beam can sing. Let me prove it as, pink-slipped,

I tremolo. You keep your bottom line,
your bloat, your silt-feeding barbels.

I'll find a new perch, wind-whipped and precarious,
directing my bellow to the brazen horizon.

The Bow Must Bear the Brunt

I point myself into the storm. Why not?
    Anyone can die in bed.

When the deck bucks and runnels white,
    I walk, clinging to ropes

and yawing like a drunkard. A staggerer,
    a vomiter, I'm not sorry.

I held a pencil once, and didn't like it,
    a clerk no more than a fly

battering glass, then dying on the sill.
    Better the rigging, the crow's nest

tucked into the sky like a navel, and me the lint
    escaping the finger.

Subtle Demonisms

All that most maddens and torments; all that stirs up the lees of things; all truth with malice in it; all that cracks the sinews and cakes the brain; all the subtle demonisms of life and thought; all evil, to crazy Ahab, were visibly personified, and made practically assailable in Moby Dick.

And what cask of vileness have you laid up,
      wicking tannins in cellar dankness? What bitter,

over-steeped brew do you drain to the lees, then tip
      to read the grit? What spread-eagles you

over the wooden hurdle, pitted with nail-marks
      from previous visits, you bent and striped,

digging in so as not to cry out, then crying out
      just the same, moaning and bleeding,

piss red-threaded? What names do you pronounce
      in your nightly mantra,
what death curse before retiring, eyes probing
      the gloom, hook-taloned and hungry

for the crunch of bones and coppery marrow?
　　　What, close at hand,

have you named proxy, scapegoat for all the hurt
　　　you can't do to the other?

Thou Did'st Not Know Ahab Then

For a Khan of the plank, and a king of the sea, and a great lord of Leviathans was Ahab.

I am ever and more myself. A stump settling
into the hole set for me, my chin tillering

weatherwards, planing the wind like a knife.
My dreams condense in their alembic

in a deepening drip. Nothing soothes,
but hithering to and fro appeases. Not

for me the small pleasures, the sucked pipe
and the cracked marrowbone. Mine, instead,

obsession's scrimshaw, whittled into a dappling
like light upon swells. Neither for me the proof

bottle with its cotton swaddle. I'd rather rasp
myself over whetstones, readying for the unseen

jugular. *Down, dog, and kennel!*
I have said, and almost come to grief for it,

but no man tells me to stifle, tamping me
like a sponged bore. I'll not be de-sparked.

Rather loaded and re-, sending red hot lances
to spume before sinking. It'll come to that,

for I've a premonition. Already, I answer
for the souls I drag behind. Bone rattling my way

to judgement, I turn down my brim, up my collar,
salt thoughts working their slow corrosion.

No Key

My soul is more than matched; she's overmanned.

There it swims, tomorrow's pearly mass, sounding
then breaching.

I have vowed to lash it fast, to master and render it,
while knowing,

every prior day, I have doused my candle
in failure.

I am not one to balance in rough water, looking
neither right nor left.

Some shadow, some noise, some inner weather
diverts me,

and the whale escapes, the broken rope another taunt
I cannot decipher.

Dismasted and Re-

Hardly have we mortals by long toilings extracted from this world's vast bulk its small but valuable sperm; and then, with weary patience, cleansed ourselves from its defilements, and learned to live here in clean tabernacles of the soul; hardly is this done, when—there she blows!—the ghost is spouted up, and away we sail to fight some other world, and go through young life's old routine again.

At night
come resolutions, *nevers* and *won'ts* pieced

laboriously,
a ship within a bottle, perfectly trimmed.

I lay out
new routes, promising not to venture *there*

or *there*.
The dawn wind flares me afresh, ribboning

bright purpose.
I will be kind, my name synonymous with

the good.
But hardly have I loosed cleats before a new storm

dismasts me.
My holystoned decks stream clotted waters.

Nothing lashed
stays put. Scrabbling for ropes, I ride it out.

Again
the battering, again the taking stock. Petrel

and albatross witness
this endless repair beneath wing-shadow.

That Imbecile Candle

There, then, he sat, holding up that imbecile candle in the heart of that almighty forlornness.

Last night, I thought – more than two-thirds through –
and felt the narrowing of the way, the sacks gone
slack with the daily taking, most of the fun
consumed, the glossy health, the heedlessness of youth.
The moon slid its cold silver on the truth
of it as I lay in my shared bed, alone
with my overloud pulse, an implacable metronome
marking, no matter how I twisted, its tune.

Yet somehow, still, I hoped for dawn,
even if it meant further diminishment, lifting,
like a befogged sailor, my tiny light, lashed
to an oar, unable to row, to keep on
course, to do anything but imagine my beacon saving
me for another day, however wave-washed.

Now You Know

> *[W]herein differ the sea and land, that a miracle upon one is not a miracle upon the other?*

Your boat founders, but you choose
not to drown. Miraculously,

the deeps bear your weight. You ride
wild currents, claiming your place

in the shoals. You are more
than a single body. Leviathan

frolics at your side, jaws
a scrimshaw of phosphorescence.

Why have you wasted any part
of your lifetime fearful

of being washed overboard?
Now you know darkness

but temporary. No void, loneliness
teems with mermaids and elvers.

The Black Bubble

Round and round, then, and ever contracting towards the button-like black bubble at the axis of that slowly wheeling circle, like another Ixion I did revolve. Till, gaining that vital center, the black bubble upward burst...

We are all made to be held,
circling what draws us
like one lashed to a wheel.

For years, I tried to wrench myself
from this dizzying center,
only to drift back, sooner or later.

Now, I let myself rest
on waves that once terrified. Only then,
does the black bubble burst.

Last Sleep

Aye, toil we how we may, we all sleep at last on the field.

I have come to the age of mortality, my father says,
his organs lit from within. He sounds like a man

playing a noble role, which is not to say insincere.
What can we do but repeat the lines of our betters

as we fall to our knees. I am no Melville but would be
happy enough to sound his echo. I listen to my dying father

and wonder how high he will set the bar. Will I, too,
have to say I saw death coming, that if not ready, I am

at least resigned to exit? *Thus*, I give up the spear, Ahab cried.
Thus, I say, and set a final period, my Pequod spiraling down.

Acknowledgments

Burning One's Own Body — *The Oakland Review*
Castaway — *Christian Century*
Fast at Both Ends — *What Rough Beast*
How Is Mortal Man to Account for It — *Cold Mountain Review*
I Go Willingly — *Rock & Sling*
Selfie — *Anti-Heroin Chic*

A number of these poems first appeared in a limited-edition chapbook from Red Flag Poetry entitled *The Bow Must Bear the Brunt*.

About the Author

Devon Balwit's work appears in *The Worcester Review*, *The Cincinnati Review*, *Tampa Review*, *Barrow Street*, *Rattle*, *Sierra Nevada Review* and *Grist* among others. Her most recent collections are *We Are Procession*, *Seismograph* (Nixes Mate Books, 2017), *Rubbing Shoulders with the Greats* (Seven Kitchens Press, 2020), and *Dog-Walking in the Shadow of Pyongyang* (Nixes Mate Books, 2021). For more, visit https://pelapdx.wixsite.com/devonbalwitpoet

42° 19' 47.9" N 70° 56' 43.9" W

Nixes Mate is a navigational hazard in Boston Harbor used during the colonial period to gibbet and hang pirates and mutineers.

Nixes Mate Books features small-batch artisanal literature, created by writers who use all 26 letters of the alphabet and then some, honing their craft the time-honored way: one line at a time.

nixesmate.pub